CLAIM YOUR STAGE

MOVE FROM STAGE FRIGHT TO SPOTLIGHT.

LOVE, BOBBIE JO

Copyright © 2021 by Love, Bobbie Jo
Edited by Gabrielle Gigot
Cover & interior designed by Aeysha Mahmood
Cover Image by FrameStockFootages/Shutterstock.com

All rights reserved. No part of this publication may be reproduced, distributed or transmitted in any form or by any means, including photocopying, recording, or other electronic or mechanical methods, without the prior written permission of the publisher, except in the case of brief quotations embodied in critical reviews and certain other noncommercial uses permitted by copyright law. For permission requests, write to the publisher, addressed "Attention: Permissions Coordinator," at
hello@lovebobbiejo.com.

Love, Bobbie Jo/All About Healing, LLC
Kewaunee, WI
LoveBobbieJo.com

Claim Your Stage/ Love, Bobbie Jo. —1st ed.
ISBN 978-1-7361210-1-6

May this book inspire you to step into the star that you are.
Love, Bobbie Jo

TABLE OF CONTENTS

FOREWARD 7

CHAPTER ONE
STAGE FRIGHT & SPOTLIGHT 9

CHAPTER TWO
VALUES 15

CHAPTER THREE
VISION 21

CHAPTER FOUR
VOICE 27

CHAPTER FIVE
VISIBILITY 33

CHAPTER SIX
VULNERABILITY 39

CHAPTER SEVEN
SET THE STAGE 45

CHAPTER EIGHT
CREATE YOUR STAGE 51

CHAPTER NINE
CLAIM YOUR STAGE 55

ABOUT THE AUTHOR 61

FOREWARD

I've spent a lot of time backstage, waiting for permission. Waiting for an invite. Waiting to be ready. Studying and rehearsing like a stand-in. What I've come to find was the only thing really holding me back from stepping out from behind the curtain was me. All I needed to do was claim my stage.

When I say "Claim Your Stage," yes, it can refer to literally being a speaker on the stage, but I'm also talking about you being YOU. With this, you construct your stage from your kitchen table, the grocery store—anywhere you step. The whole world becomes your stage (hello, Shakespeare!).

When I say, "Step into the *star that you are*," it's not about being a star in the sense of collecting accolades and receiving applause, it's about being a star in the sense that you are made of star dust! It's claiming the essence that you already are. It's no longer playing small (stage fright), but allowing yourself to shine (spotlight).

Being the star that you are and claiming your stage is sacred. It is your birthright. It is honoring the gifts you've been given and sharing them like you came here to do. It's listening within, connecting to your soul, and living your truth.

In this book, I share with you simple insights to help you make that move from stage fright to spotlight. This is an interactive journey where you get to connect, clarify and claim your stage, one page at a time.

Without further ado, grab your favorite writing tool, and let's claim the stage waiting for YOU!

Love, Bobbie Jo

CHAPTER One

To hide behind the curtain—quiet, safe, small—or to step into the light and give it my all. What if I fail? What if I fall? Oh, but even worse yet is to die knowing, I didn't embrace my call.

STAGE FRIGHT & SPOTLIGHT

From hiding to shining.

Let's start by diving into what "stage fright" and "spotlight" may look like.

STAGE FRIGHT

When we are in this state, we are hiding, playing small, performing for "should" and expectations, following the status quo, and allowing all the inner (or outer) chatter to hold us back.

This can be an uncomfortably comfortable place. A place we are used to being. Therefore, it is easy to stay behind the curtain. We may be perfecting things, feeling not ready, rebuilding, questioning and seeking more information.

It's as if we are behind the scenes getting into character, going over our lines, and feeling the nerves of a live audience. We allow all these things to stop us, pause us, and give us all the reasons that we are not ready yet.

Or, we may be simply going through the motions, being all the things we feel we need to be, while inwardly wanting to express so much more.

In our business, stage fright may appear as a feeling of not being ready until we perfect that website, get new business cards, take another course, await someone to tell us we are ready or good enough, or worry about taking a chance on what we really want to be doing.

In our personal life, stage fright may look like doing things that we really don't want to but we feel we have to do, swallowing our voice rather than speaking up, wearing things that don't light us up but are what everyone else is wearing, or not honoring who we really are but being who we feel we need to be to be accepted.

SPOTLIGHT

When we are in the spotlight state, we are owning our light, living our truth, expressing our voice, and sharing our gifts. We are living in unity with our soul, our deepest sacred essence, in its true form.

Here, we step out from behind the scenes and take our place on stage. We know our character, because it is the very essence of our being. Our role is who we are and our lines are the purity of our voice expressing our truth.

The stage is a sacred place where we get to share from our heart.

In our business, it may look like sharing our gifts, offering our services, speaking up when we have something to offer, and being excited about what we do. We take on the projects and clients that light us up, and we refer out the ones that don't.

In our personal life, it may look like saying no when we don't want to do something, using our voice to state our feelings and our truth, and being and expressing who we really are rather than trying to fit in.

WHAT I'VE LEARNED:

Living in stage fright creates the feeling of a void for me. My soul knows there is something missing. No matter how uncomfortably comfortable I get with hiding, I know my time is not here for that. I believe we are all here to shine. Therefore, in those times when I'm shrinking back in stage fright, I remind myself of the sacred calling to spotlight and make the shift. It's a journey, and well worth taking the steps to claim your stage!

Your Turn to Reflect.

On the following lines (or in your journal), take a moment to reflect on areas in your life you feel you may be in "stage fright" and where you feel you have claimed your "spotlight" (or where you would like to). When you look at the areas of stage fright, what might be some of the factors keeping you backstage? What are the possible positive outcomes in these areas if you step into spotlight?

CHAPTER
Two

A compass may guide you North, South, East or West, yet an inner knowing will take you in the direction that, for you, is best.

VALUES

Your inner compass.

The first step in moving from stage fright to spotlight is knowing your core values. These are different than morals or principals. What you're connecting with here are the qualities that are most important to you personally and your desired way of living.

Your core values are like an inner compass, an essence of your being. When you are living in harmony with them, you feel fully alive. On the flip side, when something feels off, it's most likely a sign that you are not in alignment with one of your values.

For example, my biggest core value is expression. If I am not honoring this value and expressing my voice, I feel dead inside. When I went a long period repressing my ability to express, it showed up physically as an imbalance in my body.

During this time, I was in "stage fright," playing small and swallowing my voice, rather than "spotlight," owning my voice and sharing my gifts.

When we know what our core values are, it can help us navigate life and notice when we've steered off course.

YOUR VALUES

Let's uncover your core values. Below, you will find a list of some examples. Please note, there are more than what is listed here, so if something is calling to you, write in your own!

Take a moment to read through the list, and circle any that jump out at you.

Examples

Freedom	Connection	Honesty	Curiosity
Nature	Status	Collaboration	Expression
Purpose	Adventure	Family	Nobility
Contribution	Courage	Humor	Identity
Health	Joy	Peace	Passion
Travel	Mastery	Diversity	Communication
Creativity	Learning	Growth	Security
Exploration	Leadership	Wealth	Beauty
Appreciation	Recognition	Compassion	Love
Success	Oneness	Wisdom	Trust
Harmony	Authenticity	Gratitude	Power
Serenity	Patience	Vitality	Simplicity
Friendship	Community	Generosity	Positivity
Abundance	Spirituality	Flexibility	Originality
Integrity	Service	Inspiration	Fun

Next, revisit those circled items and connect a little deeper to the word. How does it feel? Is it truly a desired feeling in your life? Something that if you weren't in rapport with, you would feel something is missing? Or, does it have you saying, "I *should* embody this more." In that case, it is known as a "should" value, not a core value. We are seeking to find the ones that are true for you.

We typically have around 4-7 core values at a time. Revisit this list until you have it narrowed close to that. Trust your intuition. If you have a little more or a little less, that's okay. You will continue connecting with them and feeling their essence.

Here are some more questions to ask if you're having trouble finding the words/essence.

What is something you dislike? Why? What is it missing?

Is there someone you greatly admire? Why? What is it about them?

When are you the happiest?

These questions can help point you to the values that you value!

WHAT I'VE LEARNED:

Having my core values as a compass helps me understand why I feel certain ways, and helps direct me on my journey to live in greater purpose and joy. When I feel something trigger or upset me, or feel down and "blah," I can check in with my values and reflect upon the situation. Am I holding something in that I really want to express? Am I dimming my light? Did one of my values get stepped on by someone, or by myself? Then, I can adjust how I need.

Your Turn to Reflect.

Use the space below to write your core values. Feel free to expand by journaling about what it looks and feels like for these values to be expressed in your life and how it looks and feels when they are not.

_____
_____
_____
_____
_____
_____
_____
_____
_____
_____
_____
_____
_____
_____
_____
_____
_____
_____
_____
_____
_____
_____
_____
_____
_____
_____
_____
_____
_____

VALUES

CHAPTER
Three

Aboard a boat, with no direction to go, the sails will abide wherever the wind does blow. Yet if your desire is not to be cast out at sea, adjust those sails to direct the wind to where you want to be.

VISION

Where do you want to go?

When we don't know where we want to go, we can easily spend time in places we don't want to be. Perhaps we are there because we think we should be, or someone else wants us there, or we're really not sure what we want because we've been meeting everyone else's needs rather than our own.

The next key in moving from stage fright to spotlight is to have a clear vision. Where do you want to go?

When I was living in a directionless place of stage fright, I allowed others to dictate where I placed my energy. I wasn't grounded in knowing my desires, so those desires became more about pleasing.

I was going through the motions making sure everyone else was happy, and I lost an essential part of myself. My core value of expression was not being honored in my vision because I had no idea what my vision was.

When I shifted my mindset to spotlight by connecting with myself and getting clear on what direction I wanted to take my business and how I wanted to feel in my personal relationships, everything transformed.

I had a clear focus. I knew where to direct my energy.

It's like being out to sea and allowing the wind to toss your sail wherever the wind may blow, versus navigating with that wind and using the sails to catch and direct it to your desired location.

This way, you can make your way to that beach you see in the distance rather than feeling lost out at sea.

When you know where you want to go, you know where to place your "no." You can create healthy boundaries that keep you aligned with your vision. For instance, when I decided to claim my vision of being an author, I knew writing was essential to living this! Therefore, when I have writing time on my calendar, or feel the inspiration hit me, and another request comes my way for that very same time slot, I know it is a "no." It is steering me away from my vision and in a direction I don't want to go.

Let's say your vision is to be a baker. You decide this. You envision it. You feel it. You know it! You start taking the steps. Then, you are approached with the request to turn your kitchen into a fast food establishment. Since you have your vision, it's clear what your answer to that request would be.

Now, say you weren't clear. You just knew you had a kitchen and wanted to do something with it. It'd be far easier to say yes to anything kitchen-related. This doesn't mean you might not bake someday, however, you could be baking much sooner if you had that clear vision first. You know where you want to place your energy—on baking. Sure, you could use it to make french fries, but if your soul calling is cakes, making french fries will eventually have you feeling fried.

Clear vision makes you the lighting technician. You get to direct the spotlight where you want on the stage, not someone else. Where do you want to illuminate and shine?

Focused energy is where the magic occurs. Perhaps you've heard the saying, energy flows where attention goes!

Think about the sun radiating upon the earth. It is vast and covering a large area. Now, when you focus some of that sunlight with a mirror or magnifying glass and channel its energy to heat dry kindling, fire can occur. This is the power of focus. Where do you want to ignite your life?

CLARIFY YOUR VISION

What are you called to be and to do? What are your dreams and desires? I invite you to take a moment and journal your ideal day. What does it look like? Write as if it is all happening now.

How do you feel when you wake up? What's the first thing you do? What are you doing with your loved ones? What are you doing in your business? Who are you working with? How do you feel throughout your day? How do you close out your day?

Write out as many details as you can. As you reflect upon this, notice if your "values" from tip one are being honored in this vision.

How this helps you move from stage fright to spotlight is by giving you that clear focus. What is calling you forward to claim your stage, rather than staying hidden behind the curtain? Where do you want to shine that spotlight?

WHAT I'VE LEARNED:

Getting clear on my vision made a world of difference. Making that "someday" idea into a "today" reality—that transformation begins with clarity. Who do I get to be to claim the stage I'm called to? I choose to be her now.

Your Turn to Reflect.

Journal your vision below.

VISION

CHAPTER
Four

I've never heard a sound so sweet. It was unfamiliar to any I've heard out on the street. It was pure, it was true, a sound that could only have come from you.

VOICE

Your unique expression.

What is your voice?

Just as each musical instrument has its individual sound, you also have a unique voice. You carry your own energy, vibration and song. Your "music" is original.

You hold a unique story, unique experiences, and a unique style. No one else has what you have, exactly how you have it. Your life and your perspective is one of a kind. Your voice is distinctive.

It's easy to stay in stage fright, hiding behind the scenes when we think all the roles have been filled. Or, we step out onto the stage and hear everyone else saying our lines, and then we shrink back down.

Even if you are saying something that has been said, it is different because it is you. There are core messages, philosophies, and ideas in the air that many are called to share. Yet, each perspective is different. What if someone said, "That song has already been played." But, it's only been played on a trumpet! What about a clarinet? Or flute?

That's the beauty of honoring our voices! Like music, even if we play the same note, we are unique-sounding instruments who have been finely tuned by our life experiences and preferences.

It is about expressing authentically and with integrity, not mimicking. It's a matter of staying true to you—sharing what you're called to say using your language, your personality, and your flair. The "music" your instrument (you!) is here to play.

No one can duplicate your voice. It is unparalleled. Even if someone may say what you say, and do what you do, the one thing they can't do— is be YOU.

Everyone is drawn to and resonates with something different. Therefore, there are people who resonate with *you*. Someone is waiting to hear what you have to say, how only you can say it.

Your voice has purpose and is needed. Your story and your message matter.

I've had many moments in stage fright, afraid to express my voice. What if it was wrong? What if no one liked it? What if I'm rejected? What will people think? Who am I to say…? What if I offend or hurt someone? Someone else already said this, so what's the point?

What that led to was silence or taking on the voice of what I believed others wanted to hear. Not my voice, but a voice that fulfilled the role of just fitting in—"yes" when I meant "no," quiet when I had something to say.

Silencing our voices doesn't serve. Taking on an unaligned voice doesn't serve. We are here to express our truth through our originality. The band is not complete until each individual instrument plays its part.

Do not silence your instrument. Do not try to play your flute like a trombone. Honor the song within you. Grace us with its sound.

Own your voice. It's beautiful. It's needed. It is what will call your ideal clients in. It is what will connect you with others. And you'll have a whole lot more fun expressing when you're being true to you! Share your unique voice.

My unique sound is a blend of poet, mermaid, island girl, drunken sailor, movie star and wise sage, to name a few. See, you can combine just about anything!

Our voices are the instruments that share what we've personally gone through, witnessed, learned, feel, think, observe, etc. It is sound and words giving language to our eyes, heart and soul.

Honor your unique sound and the notes *you* are called to play, the words *you* are called to say, the stories *you* are here to share and, most importantly, the impact you are here to make.

The world needs who YOU are. Your voice. Your story. Your message. Your gifts. Express the true you. Authenticity is music for the soul!

Use your voice to amplify your vision aligned in your values.

WHAT I'VE LEARNED:

I used to get caught up in "voice." Wishing I had a better one that could sing. Thinking it was all about my "message" and getting stuck on what is that- certainly I can't express until I'm completely clear! Having great thoughts to share then someone gets them out before me. Or sharing to find someone repeat what I've said. It all reminds me to come back to me. Maybe my voice isn't for singing (unless it's alone in the shower), but it sure loves to write! To know my voice is more than my message, it's my every day expression. And that it's in expressing our mess that we find our message to express! To always stay true to who I am regardless of what others are doing. To play the music I am here to play in the key God tuned me to.

Your Turn to Reflect.

What is a unique quality about your voice that you are ready to own? What is a message or story you feel called to share? What does your soul long to speak, and how does it wish to express?

_____
_____
_____
_____
_____
_____
_____
_____
_____
_____
_____
_____
_____
_____
_____
_____
_____
_____
_____
_____
_____
_____
_____
_____
_____
_____
_____
_____
_____

CHAPTER *Five*

The audience awaits, an impatient crowd. The theatre rattles with anticipation so loud. There are words their souls have been longing to hear, and they know the instrument is near. Pull back the curtain, step into the light. Shine your gifts, shine them bright.

VISIBILITY

Share the gift of you.

In order to claim your stage you need to be... **gasp* dare I say* ... SEEN!

Believe it or not, I am an introvert!

Oh, as much as I love the stage, I could easily stay behind the scenes... in a cozy little beach cottage writing poetry all day, and then keeping those sacred words tucked in my little notebooks, hidden from eyes other than mine.

Yet, in order to make an impact, I need to allow myself to be seen. If I hid all my gifts away, what good would they do?

I believe we are here to share who we are. Your gifts are for giving. And in order for people to know you have that gift to be received, they need to see you.

Therefore, a big part of moving from stage fright to spotlight is coming out of hiding and allowing yourself to be seen... and on more than one occasion! Consistently.

What does that look like in your business?

Let people know who you are. Let people know what you offer. Let people know where to connect with you.

When? Now. Not when something is perfect (there's no such thing). Not when you get another degree (you've got what you need). Not when your website is done (you can connect without it). Not when your business cards are ready (grab a post-it!). Now.

In your personal life, it's simply being you—dressing how you feel, speaking from your heart, honoring your boundaries (saying no when you want), and letting those around you see *you*.

Becoming visible can look a number of different ways. So, if this tip has your introverted side ready to drive off to that beach cottage, pause and ask yourself, "Which way am I comfortable starting with?"

A post on social media? An email to a friend? A video on YouTube? A call to a colleague? Saying "no" rather than keeping silent? Asking for support? Wearing that tropical shirt when everyone else is wearing a polo?

If being visible is new and scary, start small... yet stay consistent. Consistency is key. Especially in business and marketing, it takes seeing things many, many, many times for someone to actually "see" it and get it, so don't give up.

God graced you with your gifts to share, not to hide away. Grace us with the gift that you are. Your stage and your spotlight are waiting…

Get visible with your voice, in alignment with your vision and values.

WHAT I'VE LEARNED:

It is so easy to stay in hiding. I still find myself wanting to be in that beach cottage, yet I know deep down that is not what I am here for. Perhaps part of my journey, yes, is to connect with my gift and allow it to flow, but then to remember gifts are for giving. I don't want to come to the end of my time and look around me to see all the gifts I so beautifully wrapped, yet handed them to no one. A gift that could have brightened a day or transformed a life, now sits under a covering of dust. No matter how uncomfortable being seen can be at times, it's better than realizing I missed the opportunity to touch a life. I'm willing to go through the discomfort to offer someone, somewhere some comfort.

Your Turn to Reflect.

How can you step into visibility?

If you are already comfortable getting visible, where is your favorite place to connect? (social, email, youtube, etc.)

If you are just starting to get visible, where do you want to begin? (posting, emailing, calling, etc.)

How about personally? How do you like to be seen? What is your unique, visible style and persona? Are you expressing it? If not, how can you start?

_____
_____
_____
_____
_____
_____
_____
_____
_____
_____
_____
_____
_____
_____
_____
_____
_____
_____
_____

VISIBILITY

CHAPTER
Six

*A vulnerable place, to share one's soul.
Allowing others your heart to deeply know.
Yet on the stage, you are the star, and you
get to decide where to take
them and how far.*

VULNERABILITY

Your truth. Your terms.

When we decide to go from hiding behind the scenes, to stepping out into the light and claiming our stage, it can feel a little vulnerable, and it also requires us to be a little vulnerable.

What people desire is real. They want you—who you really are.

Authenticity is what connects us. We can feel when someone is being truthful and real versus when someone is performing or acting in a certain manner to receive acceptance, approval, or whatever they are seeking.

When you are in your real, raw, honest, authentic expression, your energy is in alignment with your soul. Your spotlight (you!) is shining. Your instrument (your voice and energy) is in tune.

That being said, vulnerability is on *your* terms. You get to choose what you share, who you share it with, and when you share it.

Vulnerability does not mean that you have to show up naked and share all of your deepest, darkest secrets. What I am speaking to here, is that your vulnerability is sharing the real you, as deep as you want to take people, and the people you choose to share yourself with.

You may choose to share more on your private stage (family, friends) than your public stage (business, speaking, work, etc). The key is knowing it always gets to be on your terms. You can say no to sharing when it does not feel aligned or right for you.

When I published my first book, "I Just Want To Be Me," it felt vulnerable sharing my personal story. It still does at times! Yet deeper within, I knew I wanted to make an impact with my story. In the book, I share details, but not all the details. I found what felt good to share. It was just the right amount of vulnerable for me.

When you move into your truth and into your light, and show up in service, people want and resonate with who YOU are—who you really are. Our stories connect us.

Yes, it may feel vulnerable and may require vulnerability, but always know it is on your terms.

As you step into sharing and vulnerability, one thing that helps is to focus on the spotlight—not as a spotlight shining *on* you, but as the spotlight shining *through* you. The spotlight is the truth of your essence, the sacredness of your soul. Feel your purpose behind what you share on your stage. Let the mission and message be greater than the fear. Let the courage of your heart and your Divinity, with the reminder of the briefness of this time, rise up within you to empower you while also holding you in its deep, peaceful presence.

Believe in your light. Own your voice. Claim your stage. Share your truth—on your terms.

WHAT I'VE LEARNED:

When I've received the gift of someone else's vulnerability, my life transformed. I felt less alone. I felt understood. I felt okay. This is what I remind myself when I share—that I, too, am offering that hope and that healing to another. I'm offering that connection. Even though I may feel alone in my vulnerability, I know from experience, someone out there is feeling the same and my words will offer some comfort.

Your Turn to Reflect.

How does vulnerability feel to you? How have you been vulnerable? Who and where do you feel comfortable with sharing in this way? Do you have boundaries in place to honor where that comfort line is for you?

VULNERABILITY

CHAPTER
Seven

*The character is solid. I'm clear on the plot.
I know where I'm at and all that I've got. I
use my tools and take my gifts and get them
in place for the curtain to lift.*

SET THE STAGE

Put your dream into motion.

You know where you're at. You know where you want to be. You know the tools you have at hand and the gifts you are graced with. You feel the passion in your heart.

What do you do next? Set the stage.

How does one set the stage?

Energetically and internally.

Start on the inside. Set the stage within. Connect deeply to your vision. Envision it. Feel it. Play it like a movie in your mind over and over. How does it feel to experience this desired expression? Allow that feeling to grow, stay with it, embody it, claim it!

Once you have set the internal stage, then you can begin to set the external.

This can look a number of different ways, depending on the stage you are claiming. Is it in your business? Do you want to claim to be a speaker? Claim that title on your website and business cards, in your introduction—anywhere that feels good. Start to reach out to the places you want to speak.

Is it in your personal life? Feel within what one small step to claiming that stage would be. How can you prepare the set? Is it creating space in your calendar? Is it clearing space within the home? Is it placing the journal on your bedside inviting you to write that book within you? Is it making a phone call, or writing the date on the calendar that you will? Is it saying the first "no" when you usually said "yes"?

These are just small examples. It will be unique for you and your stage.

What we do when we "set the stage" is set the energy. We are placing our intention into motion.

Take a play, for example. Preparing for a play is similar to how you put your dream into motion.

Backstage, the actor gets into character, going over their lines, getting in wardrobe and embodying the role they are to portray, just as you were doing in the first few chapters, connecting with your values, clarifying your vision and owning your voice. The actor envisions themselves delivering the performance with confidence and emotion, setting their internal stage.

Meanwhile, the stage itself is getting set with the scene. All the props are put into place to support the enacting of the play. This is what you are doing here, setting the scene, getting the stage ready to step out onto.

Finally, it all comes together as the lights dim down and the curtain goes up. The actor steps out onto stage (becoming visible and vulnerable to a live audience) and the play begins. The spotlight shines and the story is shared.

The audience receives the gift of the performance and message of the play. They walk away transformed.

Set the stage! Put the energy into motion.

WHAT I'VE LEARNED:

Setting that internal stage is paramount! There are so many things that can shake us and having that inner connection is key. The inner stage is what I come back to time and time again. It is what keeps me strong to appear on the outer stage. It helps me stay connected to my vision rather than getting distracted with what everyone else is doing.

Your Turn to Reflect.

Use the space below to journal the ways in which you can begin to set the stage! How can you set your internal stage? What things can you do to set the energy of your vision into motion? Commit to when you will take action on setting your internal and external stage.

SET THE STAGE

CHAPTER
Eight

I've waited for permission. Auditioned to be cast. Somehow my name was overpassed. Therefore I build my stage, no more to wait. I take the lead and create my fate.

CREATE YOUR STAGE

You have the power.

WHAT IS THE STAGE YOU WANT TO CLAIM?

Perhaps it is an actual stage where you want to be a speaker, a podcast you want to be interviewed on, a show you want to star in, or possibly, it's being the parent that takes their kids to the beach more often.

What this chapter is about is no longer waiting for permission or the perfect time. It is about creating it now.

Here, we are taking it another step beyond setting the stage, to actually creating the stage itself!

We are living in a day and age where we have so many more opportunities to create the vision we desire, or a variation of that vision. There are many platforms we can utilize to make our dreams a reality now—a place we can allow what is calling us forth to bloom.

Do you want a show? Create a YouTube channel and claim it!

Did you want to be on a podcast? Start one!

Do you dream of being a speaker? Create an event and speak!

Have you always wanted to be a beach mom? Grab the kids and some towels and go!

Maybe you want to be an author. Self publish!

This is what I do, and I cannot tell you how rewarding it is to go from wanting to be an author since childhood, to finally doing something about it!

This crazy little ride called life is short. Everyone is finding their place. Do not give your power to others to await permission to follow what your heart and soul is calling you to do.

Create your stage and claim it!

WHAT I'VE LEARNED:

We have so much power and capability within us. It's a matter of believing in it and applying it. As one who has waited for permission and played by all the rules, only to find myself still sitting backstage like a good girl watching everyone else get a turn, I've realized the key is within. Whose rules are you playing by? Whose permission do you seek? Grant yourself permission and create with your own rules. We can spend so much time trying to get approval, that we miss out on the truth; we only need to approve of ourselves.

Your Turn to Reflect.

Use the space below to declare the stage you are ready to create and claim! List 5 small steps you can take this month to work towards claiming your stage. Put them on the calendar. Commit to taking action on your dream.

_____
_____
_____
_____
_____
_____
_____
_____
_____
_____
_____
_____
_____
_____
_____
_____
_____
_____
_____
_____
_____
_____
_____
_____
_____
_____
_____
_____
_____

CHAPTER
Nine

*The crowd applauds and you take your bow.
Even with the nerves, you did it somehow.
Shine on, sweet star. Shine true and bright.
The world needs more of
your pure, guiding light.*

CLAIM YOUR STAGE

It's time.

TURN THE PAGE AND CLAIM YOUR STAGE!

Let's recap your journey making steps from stage fright to spotlight...

You connected with your values—the qualities you desire in life.

You clarified your vision—where is it you want to go?

You owned your voice—your unique way of expression.

You stepped into visibility—allowing yourself to be seen.

You embraced vulnerability—being true to you and sharing on your terms.

You set the stage—putting the energy of intention into motion.

You created your stage—no longer waiting for permission and embodying your desire now.

You claimed your stage—you are being you, being seen, and making your impact!

I invite you to take a moment to celebrate your dedication to self connection and clarity! You did it! This is where you take your bow, receive your applause (from your soul!) and give yourself some red carpet treatment!

As you continue shining as the star that you are, revisit these from time to time. Have your values shifted? Are you still directing your energy towards your vision? Has the vision changed? How is expressing your voice feeling and are you staying true to you? Have you started to hide behind the curtain or are you still visible on stage (side note here—taking time to recharge is welcome, vital and necessary! Just make sure to reemerge when you're ready.)? Are you staying within your comfort level in vulnerability, while continuing to share you?

WHAT I'VE LEARNED:

It's all in the decision to simply turn the page and claim your stage! You've got this. I believe in you! I'll see you on stage.

Your Turn to Reflect.

Feel free to use this space to recap your journey and experience, to declare your celebration plan, or to revisit these when you are ready.

CLAIM YOUR STAGE

ABOUT THE AUTHOR

Love, Bobbie Jo loved writing ever since she was a child, yet only used her gift and passion for self expression and personalized gifts, as she listened to the voices of the "real world" and followed many different career paths.

Foreshadowed by a poem she wrote in her childhood entitled "Lost Dreams," she eventually found herself at a crossroads, looking within to once again find who she really was.

In her first book, *I Just Want to Be Me*, Bobbie Jo shares her journey from people pleaser to personal truth.

After decades of fitting in, Bobbie Jo tossed the script, stepped into her lead role and claimed her stage. She now guides others in making the move from stage fright to spotlight.

It is her passion and purpose to be a channel of love, inspiring others in living those "lost dreams," and claiming their stage.

To discover more about Bobbie Jo, visit: lovebobbiejo.com

www.ingramcontent.com/pod-product-compliance
Lightning Source LLC
Chambersburg PA
CBHW072209100526
44589CB00015B/2445